感恩節

Customs, Traditions and Landmarks | Non-Fiction Series

Copyright © 2022 by Level Learning, INC. and Washington Yu Ying PCS™
Original and Edited Text Copyright © 2022 by Washington Yu Ying PCS™

All rights reserved. No part of this book in whole or part may be reproduced without written permission from the publisher.

Published by Level Learning, INC.
Content Contributors:
Washington Yu Ying PCS™
Level Learning - Jingyao Qi

Illustrations by: Josh Taira

Leveling classification based on Level Learning standard.
For full description, visit www.levellearning.com

ISBN 978-1-64040-028-3
Traditional Chinese Edition

About Level Learning:
Level Learning provides a literacy focused curriculum specifically designed for K-12 Chinese as a Second Language classrooms. Our program offers 20 levels of specific and detailed objectives, leveled texts and passages, mastery-based online assessment, and analytics to enable data-driven instruction. Level Learning reading curriculum for both literature and informational text emphasize grammar and comprehension skills to help teachers develop confident and independent Chinese language readers. The non-fiction series of books are specifically designed to support our informational text course based on multiple national standards. To learn more about our entire offering, visit www.levellearning.com.

About Washington Yu Ying PCS™:
Washington Yu Ying PCS is a Mandarin English dual language immersion International Baccalaureate (IB) World school. Yu Ying's mission is to inspire and prepare young people to create a better world by challenging them to reach their full potential in a nurturing Chinese/English educational environment. Yu Ying's comprehensive IB, dual immersion curriculum equips students with global competencies for success in the real world. As a leader in immersion education, Yu Ying is determined to advance Chinese language programs and global citizenry education by helping other schools create and strengthen their Chinese programs. For more information, email: products@washingtonyuying.org

十一月						
星期一	星期二	星期三	星期四	星期五	星期六	星期日
1	2	3	4	5	6	
7	8	9	10	11	12	13
14	15	16	17	18	19	20
21	22	23	(24)	25	26	27
28	29	30				

感恩節是美國的傳統節日。每年十一月的第四個星期四是美國人慶祝感恩節的日子。

這個節日為什麼被稱為「感恩節」呢?感恩節有什麼傳統呢?

1620年，一些英國人坐船來到了美洲。他們的食物很快吃光了，也有很多人來到美洲後生病死了。

這時，生活在美洲的原住民幫助了這些英國人，他們教這些英國人捕魚和種菜。

那一年的秋天，英國人和原住民的土地都大豐收了。

這些英國人感謝神讓他們平安地到達了美洲，也感謝原住民讓他們有了大豐收。

他們用火雞和南瓜做成美食來感謝原住民的幫助，所以這一天被稱為「感恩節」。直到現在，火雞和南瓜派都是感恩節的傳統食物。

現在的感恩節，人們會和家人一起慶祝，感恩美好的生活。

你們慶祝感恩節嗎？怎麼慶祝呢？

Glossary

	Pinyin	English Definition
感恩節	gǎn ēn jié	Thanksgiving
美國	měi guó	U.S.A.
傳統	chuán tǒng	tradition
節日	jié rì	festival
慶祝	qìng zhù	to celebrate
英國	yīng guó	United Kingdom
美洲	měi zhōu	North America
食物	shí wù	food
生病	shēng bìng	sick
死	sǐ	to die
原住民	yuán zhù mín	natives
捕魚	bǔ yú	to fish
種菜	zhòng cài	to grow crops
秋天	qiū tiān	autumn
豐收	fēng shōu	to harvest

	Pinyin	English Definition
感謝	gǎn xiè	thanks
神	shén	God
平安	píng ān	safely
到達	dào dá	to arrive
火雞	huǒ jī	turkey
南瓜	nán guā	pumpkin
美好	měi hǎo	good, wonderful
生活	shēng huó	life

www.ingramcontent.com/pod-product-compliance
Lightning Source LLC
Chambersburg PA
CBHW041222070526
44584CB00001B/60